ANGER Free CHALLENGE

Be the Peace JOURNAL

Also by Jacquelyn Lynn

Seven Day Anger Free Challenge

Choices (A Joyful Cup Story)

Finding Joy in the Morning: You can make it through the night

Words to Work By: 31 devotions for the workplace based on the Book of Proverbs

The Simple Facts About Self-Publishing: What indie publishers need to know to produce a great book

Work as Worship: How Your Labor Becomes Your Legacy

How to Survive an Active Shooter: What You do Before, During and After an Attack Could Save Your Life

Faith Words: Color the Words that Inspire You Every Day

Christian Meditations

ANGER Free CHALLENGE

Be the Peace

JOURNAL

Jacquelyn Lynn

Tuscawilla Creative Services • Winter Springs, FL USA
CreateTeachInspire.com

For bulk orders, contact info@contacttcs.com.

ISBN: 978-1-941826-44-7

THE ANGER FREE PRAYER

Help me to recognize situations that trigger my anger before I get angry.

Give me the strength I need to respond to anger triggers with peace, forgiveness, and love.

Make me better so that I may make the world around me better.

HOW TO USE THIS JOURNAL

If you've read *Seven Day Anger Free Challenge*, you're familiar with the structure of this journal.

You have four pages for each day. Begin in the morning with your commitment statement and a prayer. Your commitment statement is a promise you make to yourself for that day. You may use the anger free prayer from the preceding page or write a prayer of your own.

The second and third pages are for your reflections. Write these during the day as they come to you or at the end of the day. The writing prompt for each day is a suggestion to get you started. Respond to it or not, based on your experiences and feelings from the day.

The fourth page is for your plan to remain anger free and carry this life-changing message into tomorrow. In addition to general statements, you may find it helpful to list some specific actions you intend to take. Write this before you go to bed and use it the next morning to craft your commitment and prayer for the day.

This is *your* journal. Don't worry about being right or wrong—use this journal in the way that best helps you on your anger free journey.

My Commitment for Today

My Prayer to Start the Day

Reflections

The most memorable thing that happened today was:

Be the Peace

My Plan for Tomorrow

"There are two things a person should
never be angry at: what they can help, and
what they cannot."

— *Plato*

My Commitment for Today

My Prayer to Start the Day

Reflections

Here is how today was different from yesterday:

Be the Peace

My Plan for Tomorrow

> And "don't sin by letting anger control you." Don't let the sun go down while you are still angry, for anger gives a foothold to the devil. *(Ephesians 4:26-27)*

My Commitment for Today

My Prayer to Start the Day

Reflections

I was able to model being anger free today. Here's what happened:

Be the Peace

My Plan for Tomorrow

> If you kick a stone in anger, you'll hurt your own foot.
>
> *Korean Proverb*

My Commitment for Today

My Prayer to Start the Day

Reflections

I came up with a plan for dealing with my top two anger triggers today.

Be the Peace

My Plan for Tomorrow

A gentle answer deflects anger, but harsh words make tempers flare. *(Proverbs 15:1)*

My Commitment for Today

My Prayer to Start the Day

Reflections

I felt God's presence, helping me with the Anger Free Challenge, when these things happened:

Be the Peace

My Plan for Tomorrow

> "Life appears to me too short to be spent in nursing animosity or registering wrongs."
> — *Charlotte Bronte*

My Commitment for Today

My Prayer to Start the Day

Reflections

I experienced the following emotions that could have turned into anger but didn't:

Be the Peace

My Plan for Tomorrow

A hot-tempered person starts fights; a cool-tempered person stops them. *(Proverbs 15:18)*

My Commitment for Today

My Prayer to Start the Day

Reflections

My relationship with my close family members has changed in this way:

Be the Peace

My Plan for Tomorrow

My Commitment for Today

My Prayer to Start the Day

Reflections

Now that I've had a chance to think about it, here's what I learned from yesterday:

Be the Peace

My Plan for Tomorrow

Short-tempered people do foolish things, and schemers are hated. *(Proverbs 14:17)*

My Commitment for Today

My Prayer to Start the Day

Reflections

Today I told someone about the Anger Free Challenge. Here's what happened:

Be the Peace

My Plan for Tomorrow

My Commitment for Today

My Prayer to Start the Day

Reflections

Here's how what happened today is going to help me tomorrow:

Be the Peace

My Plan for Tomorrow

> But now is the time to get rid of anger, rage, malicious behavior, slander, and dirty language. *(Colossians 3:8, NLT)*

My Commitment for Today

My Prayer to Start the Day

Reflections

I felt God helping me turn away from anger when the following things happened:

Be the Peace

My Plan for Tomorrow

"Angry men are blind and foolish, for reason at such a time takes flight and, in her absence, wrath plunders all the riches of the intellect, while the judgment remains the prisoner of its own pride."

– Pietro Aretino

My Commitment for Today

My Prayer to Start the Day

Reflections

Dealing with my anger triggers before I get angry is becoming a habit.

Be the Peace

My Plan for Tomorrow

"While seeking revenge, dig two graves
– one for yourself."

– Douglas Horton

My Commitment for Today

My Prayer to Start the Day

Reflections

I think people are noticing something different about me because:

Be the Peace

My Plan for Tomorrow

"Anger makes us all stupid."
– *Johanna Spyri*

My Commitment for Today

My Prayer to Start the Day

Reflections

Today I used the following techniques to stop an anger trigger from escalating into anger:

Be the Peace

My Plan for Tomorrow

My Commitment for Today

My Prayer to Start the Day

Reflections

I left this behind today:

Be the Peace

My Plan for Tomorrow

Stop being angry! Turn from your rage! Do not lose your temper—it only leads to harm. *(Psalm 37:8)*

My Commitment for Today

My Prayer to Start the Day

Reflections

As I have turned away from anger, my joy has increased in these ways:

Be the Peace

My Plan for Tomorrow

Love is patient and kind. Love is not jealous or boastful or proud or rude. It does not demand its own way. It is not irritable, and it keeps no record of being wronged. *(1 Corinthians 13:4-5)*

My Commitment for Today

My Prayer to Start the Day

Reflections

Here's what happened today that gave me strength:

Be the Peace

My Plan for Tomorrow

My Commitment for Today

My Prayer to Start the Day

Reflections

God guided me through a difficult situation today. Here's what happened:

Be the Peace

My Plan for Tomorrow

Get rid of all bitterness, rage, anger, harsh words, and slander, as well as all types of evil behavior. *(Ephesians 4:31)*

My Commitment for Today

My Prayer to Start the Day

Reflections

Here are the situations I handled well today:

Be the Peace

My Plan for Tomorrow

"In times of great stress or adversity, it's always best to keep busy, to plow your anger and your energy into something positive."
— *Lee Iacocca*

My Commitment for Today

My Prayer to Start the Day

Reflections

This is what happened today that I will remember forever:

Be the Peace

My Plan for Tomorrow

"Mankind must remember that peace is not God's gift to his creatures; peace is our gift to each other."

– Elie Wiesel

My Commitment for Today

My Prayer to Start the Day

Reflections

My biggest challenge today was:

Be the Peace

My Plan for Tomorrow

"You have heard that our ancestors were told, 'You must not murder. If you commit murder, you are subject to judgment.' But I say, if you are even angry with someone, you are subject to judgment! If you call someone an idiot, you are in danger of being brought before the court. And if you curse someone, you are in danger of the fires of hell. *(Matthew 5:21-22)*

My Commitment for Today

My Prayer to Start the Day

Reflections

Here's what the Anger Free Challenge has helped me discover about myself:

Be the Peace

My Plan for Tomorrow

Again I say, don't get involved in foolish, ignorant arguments that only start fights. *(2 Timothy 2:23)*

My Commitment for Today

My Prayer to Start the Day

Reflections

Here's how people react to me since I accepted the Anger Free Challenge:

Be the Peace

My Plan for Tomorrow

My Commitment for Today

My Prayer to Start the Day

Reflections

My relationship with my work colleagues has improved in these ways:

Be the Peace

My Plan for Tomorrow

My Commitment for Today

My Prayer to Start the Day

Reflections

Now that I am not getting angry, I am more productive in these ways:

Be the Peace

My Plan for Tomorrow

"Anger is an acid that can do more harm to the vessel in which it is stored than to anything on which it is poured."
– *Mark Twain*

My Commitment for Today

My Prayer to Start the Day

Reflections

I need to leave this behind:

Be the Peace

My Plan for Tomorrow

> The LORD passed in front of Moses, calling out, "Yahweh! The LORD! The God of compassion and mercy! I am slow to anger and filled with unfailing love and faithfulness. *(Exodus 34:6)*

My Commitment for Today

My Prayer to Start the Day

Reflections

Here's how I've changed since I began the Anger Free Challenge:

Be the Peace

My Plan for Tomorrow

My Commitment for Today

My Prayer to Start the Day

Reflections

Here's how accepting the Anger Free Challenge has improved my health:

Be the Peace

My Plan for Tomorrow

In every place of worship, I want men to pray with holy hands lifted up to God, free from anger and controversy. *(1 Timothy 2:8, NLT)*

My Commitment for Today

My Prayer to Start the Day

Reflections

The most meaningful thing that happened today was:

Be the Peace

My Plan for Tomorrow

My Commitment for Today

My Prayer to Start the Day

Reflections

Here's how my choice to not get angry is affecting the people around me:

____

____

____

____

____

____

____

____

____

____

____

____

____

____

____

____

____

____

____

____

____

____

Be the Peace

My Plan for Tomorrow

> When you follow the desires of your sinful nature, the results are very clear: sexual immorality, impurity, lustful pleasures, idolatry, sorcery, hostility, quarreling, jealousy, outbursts of anger, selfish ambition, dissension, division, envy, drunkenness, wild parties, and other sins like these. Let me tell you again, as I have before, that anyone living that sort of life will not inherit the Kingdom of God. *(Galatians 5:19-21)*

My Commitment for Today

My Prayer to Start the Day

Reflections

The most difficult thing for me in living the Anger Free Challenge has been:

Be the Peace

My Plan for Tomorrow

My Commitment for Today

My Prayer to Start the Day

Reflections

I could have handled these situations better:

Be the Peace

My Plan for Tomorrow

My Commitment for Today

My Prayer to Start the Day

Reflections

Here's how I now deal with things that used to make me angry:

Be the Peace

My Plan for Tomorrow

My Commitment for Today

My Prayer to Start the Day

Reflections

The Anger Free Challenge has made the following permanent changes in my life:

Be the Peace

My Plan for Tomorrow

My Commitment for Today

My Prayer to Start the Day

Reflections

I could have gotten revenge on someone today, but I chose not to.

Be the Peace

My Plan for Tomorrow

"Anger is a killing thing: it kills the man who angers, for each rage leaves him less than he had been before—it takes something from him."
— *Louis L'Amour*

My Commitment for Today

My Prayer to Start the Day

Reflections

Here's what I learned about myself today:

Be the Peace

My Plan for Tomorrow

My Commitment for Today

My Prayer to Start the Day

Reflections

The Anger Free Challenge has made me stronger and better in these ways:

Be the Peace

My Plan for Tomorrow

My Commitment for Today

My Prayer to Start the Day

Reflections

Today I was able to help someone else deal with their anger. Here's what happened:

Be the Peace

My Plan for Tomorrow

Dear friends, never take revenge. Leave that to the righteous anger of God. For the Scriptures say, "I will take revenge; I will pay them back," says the LORD. *(Romans 12:19)*

My Commitment for Today

My Prayer to Start the Day

Reflections

I have a deeper understanding of anger and the damage it does than ever before.

Be the Peace

My Plan for Tomorrow

"Anger is a wind which blows out
the lamp of the mind."
— *Robert Green Ingersoll*

My Commitment for Today

My Prayer to Start the Day

Reflections

I prayed for the following people today:

Be the Peace

My Plan for Tomorrow

Don't befriend angry people or associate with hot-tempered people, or you will learn to be like them and endanger your soul. *(Proverbs 22:24-25)*

My Commitment for Today

My Prayer to Start the Day

Reflections

Today's most important lesson was:

Be the Peace

My Plan for Tomorrow

"Holding on to anger is like grasping a hot coal with the intent of throwing it at someone else; you are the one who gets burned."

— *Buddha*

My Commitment for Today

My Prayer to Start the Day

Reflections

Here's what I gained today by not getting angry:

Be the Peace

My Plan for Tomorrow

My Commitment for Today

My Prayer to Start the Day

Reflections

Here's what happened today that made me feel good:

Be the Peace

My Plan for Tomorrow

"Whatever is begun in anger ends in shame."

— Benjamin Franklin

My Commitment for Today

My Prayer to Start the Day

Reflections

Here's how I helped someone else let go of their anger:

Be the Peace

My Plan for Tomorrow

My Commitment for Today

My Prayer to Start the Day

Reflections

Here why I love my anger free life:

Be the Peace

My Plan for Tomorrow

Jacquelyn Lynn finds joy in serving others through her writing.

Her more than 40 books include *Finding Joy in the Morning: You* can *make it through the night* (companion books: *Finding Joy Journal, Finding Joy Adult Coloring Book,* and *Intentional Joy Study Guide*); *Words to Work By: 31 devotions for the workplace based on the book of Proverbs*; and *Choices,* the first novel in the Joyful Cup Story series.

Jacquelyn is also the author of *The Simple Facts About Self-Publishing: What indie publishers need to know to produce a great book.* Jacquelyn partners with her husband, Jerry Clement, on their book projects as well as on ghostwriting and producing books for clients. Together they created two Christian coloring books for adults, *Christian Meditations* and *Faith Words.*

To learn more about Jacquelyn, visit **CreateTeachInspire.com**. You can sign up to receive her weekly inspirational messages and find links to connect with her on social media.

Available online or ask your favorite local bookstore to order it for you.

The Finding Joy Collection

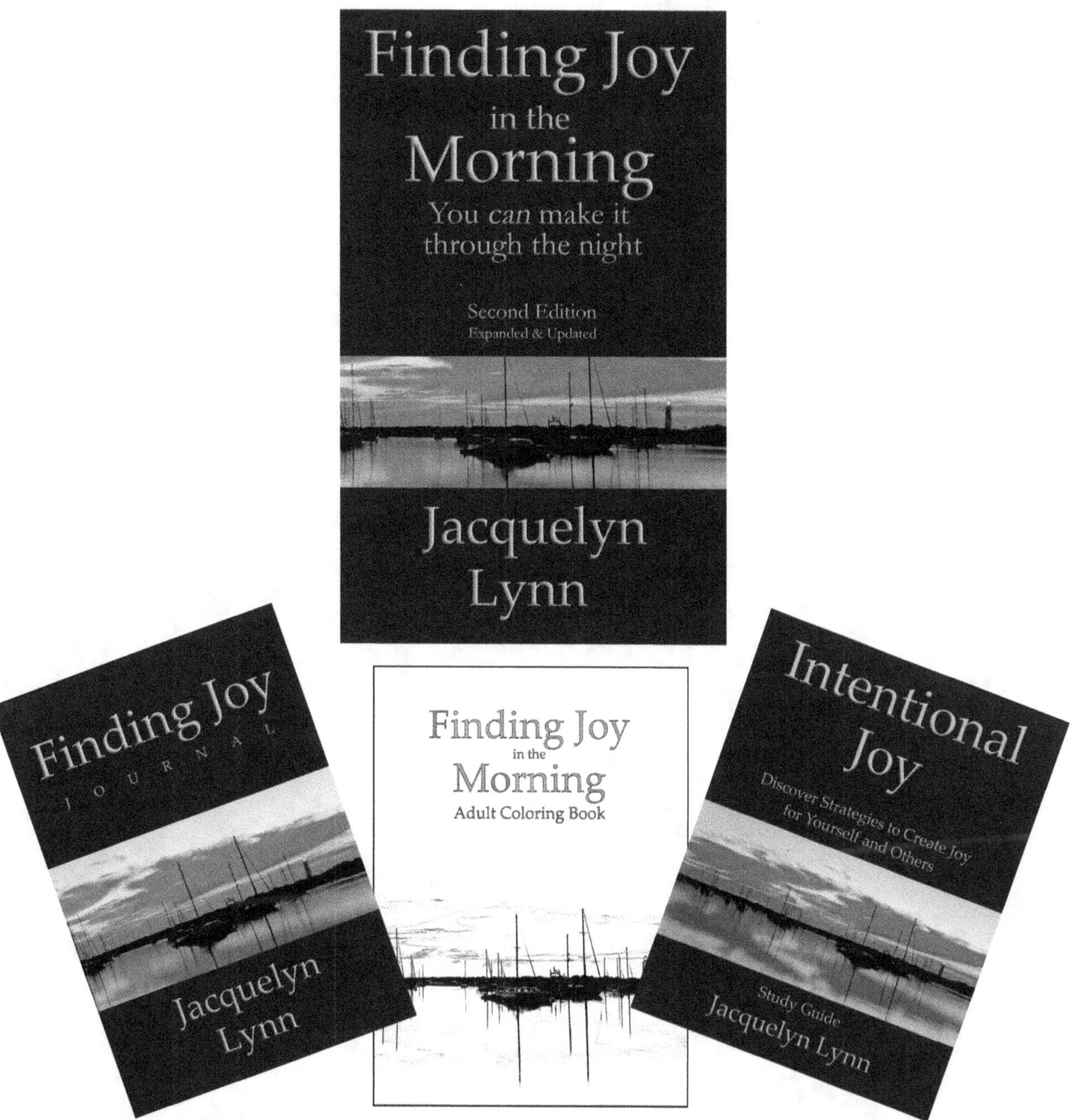

**Simple but powerful strategies to help you meet life's
toughest challenges and find joy *every* morning.**

Available online or order through your favorite local bookstore.

A single moment
The wrong choice
Lives change ...
forever.

Available on Amazon and wherever fine books are sold.

Color Your Faith

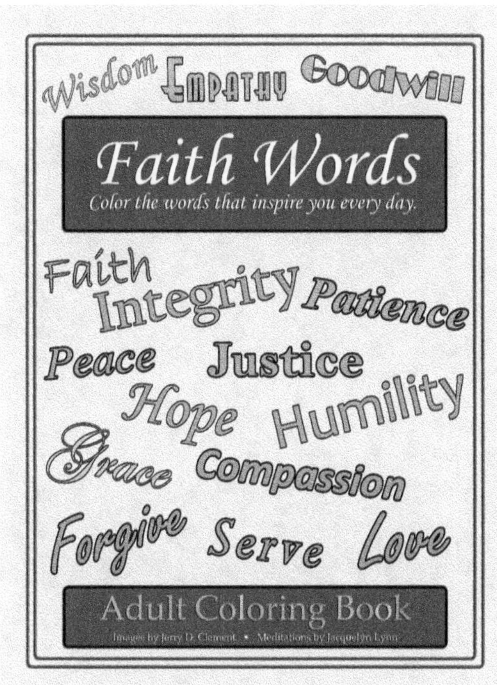

Available online or order through your favorite local bookstore.

Messages of inspiration and motivation based on the teachings of the world's greatest business advisor: King Solomon.

Devotions ideal for beginning your work day, opening a meeting, or just taking a break.

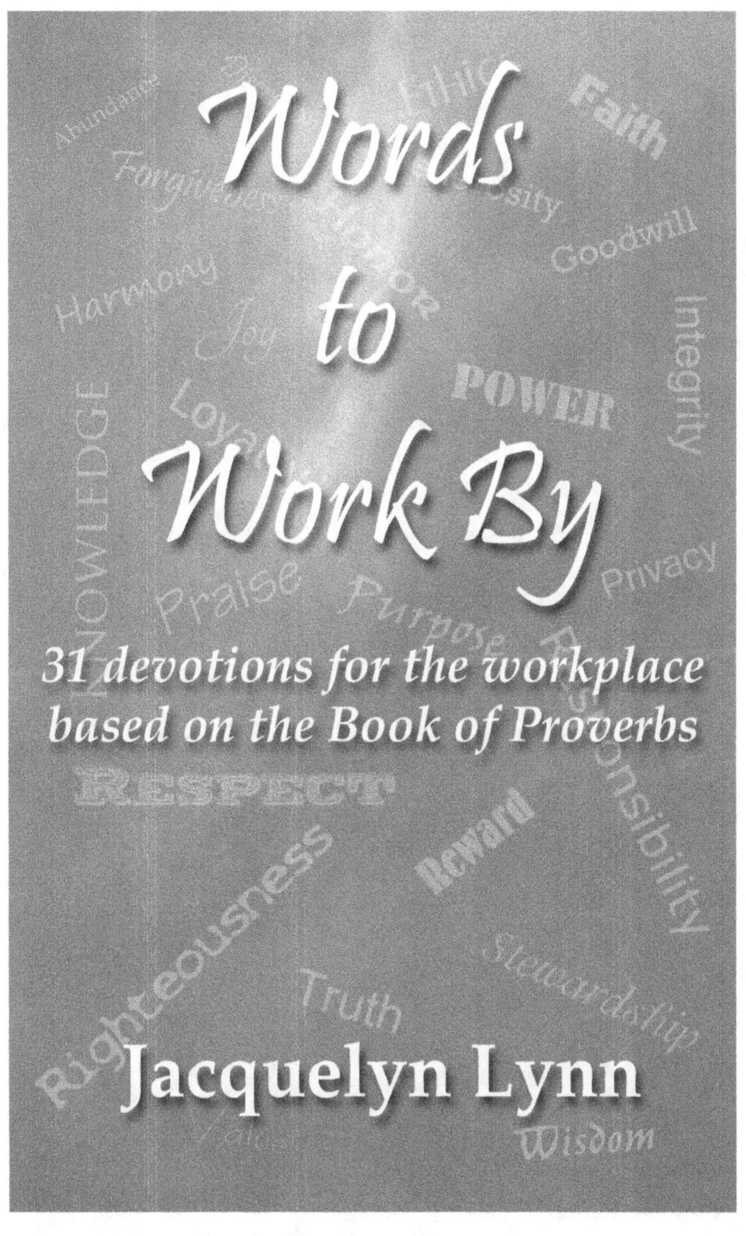

Available on Amazon and all online book retailers.

Is writing and publishing a book on your bucket list?

Find out what it takes to produce a quality book that will delight your audience and meet your goals.

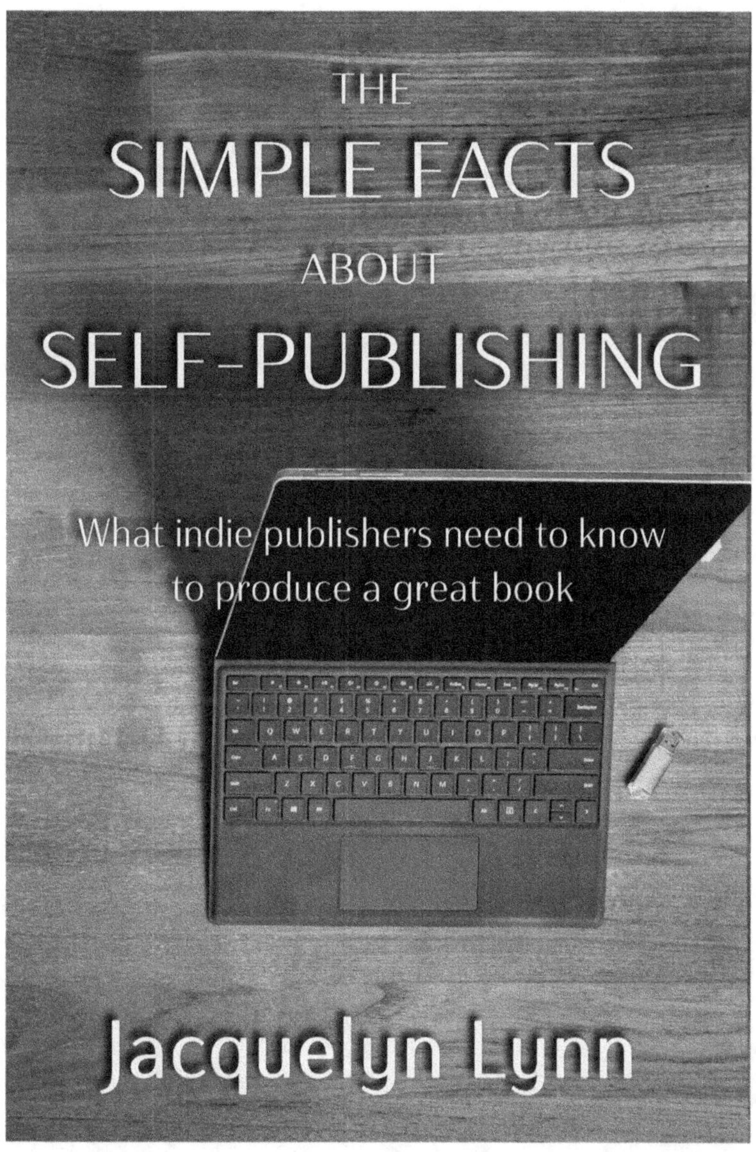

Available online or order through your favorite local bookstore.